# the giggle tent

## li taant giggle

## la tente giggle

Written by Cindy Gaudet
Illustrated by Jennifer Brown

**The Giggle Tent**

ISBN: **978-1-990818-28-8**
© Cindy Gaudet 2025



Requests for permission to make copies of any part of this work should
be submitted online at www.motherbutterfly.com

**Dedication**

CG: The River Women then, now and later.

JB: My mother who always supported me and my father who was always proud.

# Acknowledgements

The Giggle Tent was inspired by my experience of co-leading with Lii Faam Michif, Christine Tournier, Angela Rancourt and Cheryl Troupe. We are part of the River Women Collective who hosted the final ceremony of Walking With Our Sisters (WWOS) in 2019. This took place on our ancestral Métis river lands in Batoche, Saskatchewan. The WWOS ceremonial exhibit led by Métis artist, Christi Belcourt, honours the lives of Missing and Murdered Indigenous women and their families. In the way of looking after ourselves, we, four co-leads created a safe and loving physical space that we named "The Giggle Tent". The story and art celebrates our Michif way of being and doing and interrupts anything inferior about who we are.

A big maarsii to Wilfred Burton's mentorship and love of Métis stories, for Doris McDougall, Phyllis Vermette and Angela Rancourt commitment to place-based Michif language and Danielle Charest for the French translation. Thanks to SILR (Supporting Indigenous Languages Revitalization), SSRHC (Social Sciences Research Humanities Council) and Parks Canada Batoche for investing in Lii Faam Michif's creative work.

the giggle tent is a magical place

li taant giggle ay enn plaas mazhii

la tente giggle est un lieu magique

it celebrates our river life as michif people

oh we love our beautiful south saskatchewan river

she is our sister

li taant giggle oneur nutr vii michif avek la rivyar

on emm nutr bell rivyayr saskatchewan

ell ay nutr seur

elle célèbre notre vie avec la rivière en tant que
peuple michif

ohhh comme nous aimons notre belle rivière
saskatchewan sud

elle est notre sœur

we chose this place for our giggle tent because she
takes care of us

on praand set plaas akooz li taant giggle praan
swaen di nutr vii

nous avons choisi cet endroit pour notre tente
giggle parce qu'elle prend soin de nous

there was a time when we learned the stories of
our old people of how to take care of ourselves,
our family, and our land



il y a eu un temps où nous avons appris les
histoires de nos aînées sur comment prendre soin
de nous-mêmes, de notre famille, et de notre terre

at night when the stars sparkle like fireflies, we
told all kinds of little and big stories

li swary kaan lii zitwell brille koom lii moosh a
feu, on partaazh toot sort d'histwayr

le soir, quand les étoiles brillent comme les
lucioles, on racontait toutes sortes d'histoires,
petites et grandes.

we also walk
pray
and dance
together


ipi on marsh
on prii
ipi on daans
aansaamb


puis on marche
prie
et danse
ensemble

and we work together

pi on traavayl aansaamb

et on travaille ensemble

we hold on to each other until one of us
giggles, then we all smile

on s'chaen lii aen lii zoot zhusk ataan
aen di nozautr s'poof a riɥr, ipi on soorii
toot aansaamb

on se tient fort ensemble jusqu'à ce que
l'une de nous rigole, puis nous sourions
tous

WALKING
Our
SISTERS

we share about the happy moments
and carry them with us

on pataarzh lii momaan contaan ipi on
lii amen avek nozautr

on partage les moments heureux
et on les porte avec nous

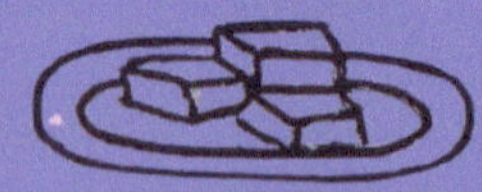

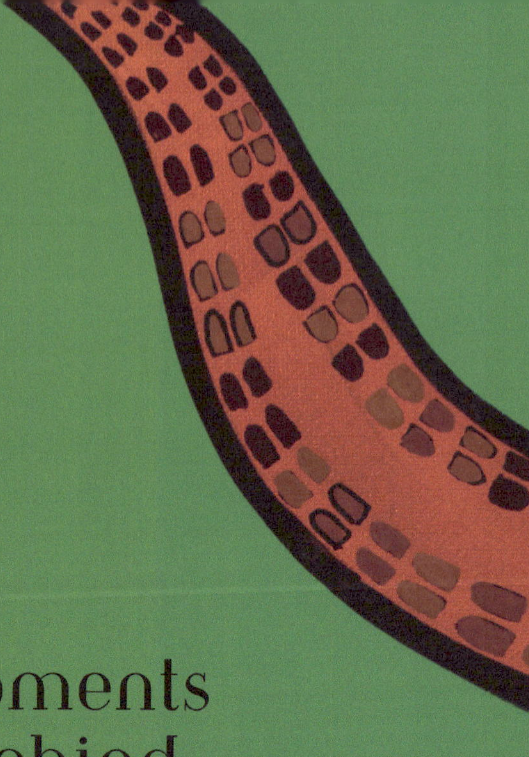

we feel our sad moments
and leave them behind

on pataarzh lii momaan paysan daan
noot keur ipi on lii layss aen aryayr

on ressent nos moments tristes
puis on les laisse derrière nous

we say it as it is
no fluff
no puff
and no muss
like our bird kin

on l'dji koom kis say
paa d'elaa ipi
paa de bavaardaghz
poor ariiyenn

on dit les choses
comme elles sont
sans détour
sans fla-fla
et sans chichi

in the giggle tent there is no boss
we walk together and help each other
feet on ground


daan li tent giggle toot li moond son
mytr deu maaime
on maarsh aansaamb pi on s'entrayd
avek lii pyi atayr


dans la tente giggle il n'y a pas de chef
on marche ensemble et on s'entraide
les pieds sur terre

we create gifts for our family and
celebrate that we are one of a kind

on emm ferr di cadoo poor nutr faamii
pi fayt konnay pas toot paray

nous créons des cadeaux pour notre
famille et nous célébrons le fait que
nous sommes tous uniques au monde

our grandmothers
mothers and aunties
help us along the way

nos maymairs
nos maamaas
pi nos mataants nouzaid

nos grand-mères
mères et tantes
nous aident au long du chemin

they walk together
like the time we lived as sister
communities


ill maarsh aansaamb
koom kaen lii michif sontay organisii
aen koomunitay di seurs


elles marchent ensemble
comme au temps où nous vivions en
communautés sœurs

oh how we love to visit
in our michif ways
can you feel how magical
the giggle tent is?

ahh on emm baen nutr bonn vii michif.
peutchu wayr la mazhii
di li taant giggle?

oh comme nous aimons se visiter
dans nos manières michifs
peux-tu sentir la magie
de la tente giggle?

# Jennifer Brown

Jennifer Brown is a Metis woman born and raised in Prince Albert, Saskatchewan. Her ancestry is directly tied to the Red River Settlement in Manitoba; when her family settled in Saskatchewan they resided in the St. Louis and Gerrond area.

Jennifer is a graduate of the Saskatchewan Urban Native Teachers Education Program in Prince Albert. Since her convocation through the University of Saskatchewan SUNTEP program she  has been working with the Saskatchewan Rivers Public School Division in Prince Albert. She has been teaching primarily middle years and high school with a specific focus on Arts Education. Jennifer is a local artist who participates in the local downtown art walk program. Her art style is based on Indigenous culture with a specific focus on Metis culture. Primarily, she develops three types of art; acrylic pointillism, traditional beadwork, and ink based Indigenous animal art that tells a story.

# Cindy Gaudet

I am an Auntie, Sister, Daughter, Grand-daughter, Niece and a Kokum. I belong to a strong lineage of Métis women's families along the South Saskatchewan River and farming communities near Bellevue, Batoche, St. Laurent, St. Louis and Hoey, Saskatchewan. I have ties to the French-Canadian relations through my father's family. I am part of the River Women Collective, and I am an Associate Professor at Campus Saint-Jean, University of Alberta. Métis women's expression of sovereignty and resistance as love, with a focus on the cultural role of Auntie, is the research and stories I am mostly passionate about.

# THE GIGGLE TENT
# LEARNING GUIDE

Learning Guide created by Kimberley Fraser-Airhart

The Giggle Tent is based on an authentic community story celebrating Métis women's kinship, love, cultural identity and Michif language learning. The activities provided can be integrated in and beyond classroom settings, and adapted to all learning levels.

## MÉTIS UNDERSTANDINGS: MICHIF

Métis are a proud, distinct Indigenous group within the lands known today as Canada. One of the distinct languages of the Métis Peoples is Michif, a living language that varies depending on the community one finds themselves connected to, or, visiting. Michif, also recognized as a cultural identity, know themselves by the lands and kinship they are rooted within. The relationships of place and people influence the variations of the Michif language.

This book centers Michif-French as part of the author's place and kinship research. The Michif featured in the Giggle Tent has roots in the Batoche, St Laurent, St Louis, Bellevue, Hoey and Duck Lake homelands of the Métis Peoples. This variation can also be heard in other Métis communities who have interconnections with Francophone relations.

It is important to honor and celebrate that there are many variations in how Michif is spoken and lived across the Métis Homelands.

## LEARNING CONNECTIONS

Scan the code or access the links below to explore activities that support classroom learning outcomes and beyond:

http://www.motherbutterfly.com/

https://sites.google.com/ualberta.ca/cindygaudet/

Our stories are penned to tickle the funny-bone, nourish the mind, & open the heart. **That's what makes our books different, and why you'll love reading them.**

Visit www.motherbutterfly.com for free books!

www.ingramcontent.com/pod-product-compliance
Lightning Source LLC
Chambersburg PA
CBHW042125030726
47599CB00002B/353